LED ZEPPELIN
HOUSES OF THE HOLY

Alfred's Platinum Album Editions

Produced by
Alfred Music Publishing Co., Inc.
P.O. Box 10003
Van Nuys, CA 91410-0003
alfred.com

Printed in USA.

No part of this book shall be reproduced, arranged, adapted, recorded, publicly performed, stored in a retrieval system, or transmitted by any means without written permission from the publisher. In order to comply with copyright laws, please apply for such written permission and/or license by contacting the publisher at alfred.com/permissions.

ISBN-10: 0-7390-6136-4
ISBN-13: 978-0-7390-6136-7

HOUSES OF THE HOLY

Houses of the Holy is perhaps the most light-hearted album in the entire Led Zeppelin catalog. With the exception of the moody "No Quarter," the 40-minute recording is frothy, celebratory, and energetic, and with good reason: 1973, the year of its release, was a very good moment in history for singer Robert Plant, guitarist Jimmy Page, bassist John Paul Jones, and drummer John Bonham.

Riding high from their previous album, 1971's *Led Zeppelin IV*, which spawned mega anthems like "Stairway to Heaven" and "Rock and Roll," the band had become rock's biggest draw, eclipsing even The Rolling Stones and The Who. A show in Tampa, Florida, shattered the single-concert attendance record set by The Beatles in 1965, and Zeppelin now flew from gig to gig on their own luxury jet with the band's logo emblazoned on its sides.

Songs like the reggae-influenced "D'yer Mak'er" and the off-kilter, funk tune "The Crunge" allowed Zeppelin's sense of humor to shine through their usual stew of raw sex, mysticism, and American blues, representing something of a stylistic turning point for the band. In fact, the blues, which was a huge part of the band's early work, is all but absent on *Houses*.

In many ways, *Houses of the Holy* is one of Zeppelin's most progressive albums, thanks to sprawling compositions like the shimmering opening track, "The Song Remains the Same," which features several tempo changes and some of Page's most dazzling guitar work. The intricate nature of some arrangements was perhaps due to the fact that several of the songs were demoed at the personal studios of Page and Jones, both of whom had recently installed recording facilities in their

John Bonham performing live at Madison Square Garden, July 29, 1973, during filming for *The Song Remains the Same*.

Robert Plant onstage at Madison Square Garden, July 29, 1973, during filming for *The Song Remains the Same*.

homes. Jimmy presented almost complete arrangements of "The Rain Song" and "Over the Hills and Far Away," while Jones offered "No Quarter." The extra thought and time is reflected on all three compositions, which feature dense arrangements and more overdubs than the group's previous recordings.

"My main goal on *Houses of the Holy* was to just keep rolling," says Page, who also produced the album. "It's very dangerous to try and duplicate yourself. I won't name any names, but I'm sure you've heard bands that endlessly repeat themselves. After four or five albums they just burn up. With us, you never knew what was coming. I think you can really hear the fun we had on *Houses*…and you can also hear the dedication and commitment."

Zeppelin even lightened their attitude toward the press. As odd as it may seem now, rock critics had not been particularly kind to the band in its early years, dismissing it as a "one-dimensional heavy rock group." While *Led Zeppelin IV* went quite a long way in softening that opinion, many rock writers were still not convinced.

In the past, Led Zeppelin had simply ignored the bad press. But as this was the dawn of a new era for them, they decided to hire Solters & Roskin, an old-school show-biz public relations firm, to help them change this unfair characterization. Danny Goldberg, Solters & Roskin's "resident long-haired rock and roller," was elected to represent the band, and he immediately set about making the world aware of what so many rock fans already knew: Led Zeppelin ruled!

"They were not critically embraced when they first came out," Goldberg says. "The critics loved Eric Clapton and Jeff Beck, and they considered Jimmy Page to be somewhat of an interloper. The press had hurt the band's feelings. But Zeppelin became instant superstars in the United States due to FM radio airplay and their incredible live shows, and they felt they didn't need print recognition.

"When I started working for them, they were working on *Houses of the Holy*, and they were in a different frame of mind. They wanted a

Robert Plant and Jimmy Page at Madison Square Garden, July 29, 1973, during filming for *The Song Remains the Same*.

fresh start and sensed it was a new chapter in the band's history and that it was time to reach a wider public."

Goldberg soon discovered that between the private jets, the rock and roll lifestyle, and the sold-out shows, Zeppelin were magnets for press coverage. But as far as their musicianship was concerned, all he had to do was report the truth.

"The main reason Zeppelin is great is because all four members of the band are incredibly talented," he says. "You could've built an entire band around any of the four of them. John Paul Jones, for example, was the least well known, and any band would've killed to have him. There's no question that John Bonham was the greatest rock drummer who ever lived. And Robert turned out to be an amazing frontman, lyricist, and singer.

"But the real key is Jimmy, who masterminded the band. He had so much confidence in his own abilities that he had no problem surrounding himself with these incredible players. Jimmy also had a vision of what was going on in rock and roll at the time and how to take it to the next level. After the '60s, Zeppelin were the beginning of the next chapter."

Although *Houses of the Holy* received some mixed reviews, many of them leveled at the tongue-in-cheek nature of some of the tracks, Zeppelin had once again remained uniquely true to themselves, and their devoted followers loved them for it. The album entered the U.K. chart at No. 1, while in the United States, its 39-week run on *Billboard*'s Top 40 was the longest since the ascent of Zeppelin's first album four years earlier.

BRAD TOLINSKI
Editor-in-Chief, *Guitar World* magazine

Robert Plant, John Paul Jones, and Jimmy Page performing live onstage at the K.B. Hallen, in Copenhagen, Denmark, March 2, 1973.

HOUSES OF THE HOLY

CONTENTS

TITLE	PAGE
The Song Remains the Same	7
The Rain Song	13
Over the Hills and Far Away	16
The Crunge	18
Dancing Days	20
D'yer Mak'er	24
No Quarter	27
The Ocean	30

DRUM NOTATION KEY

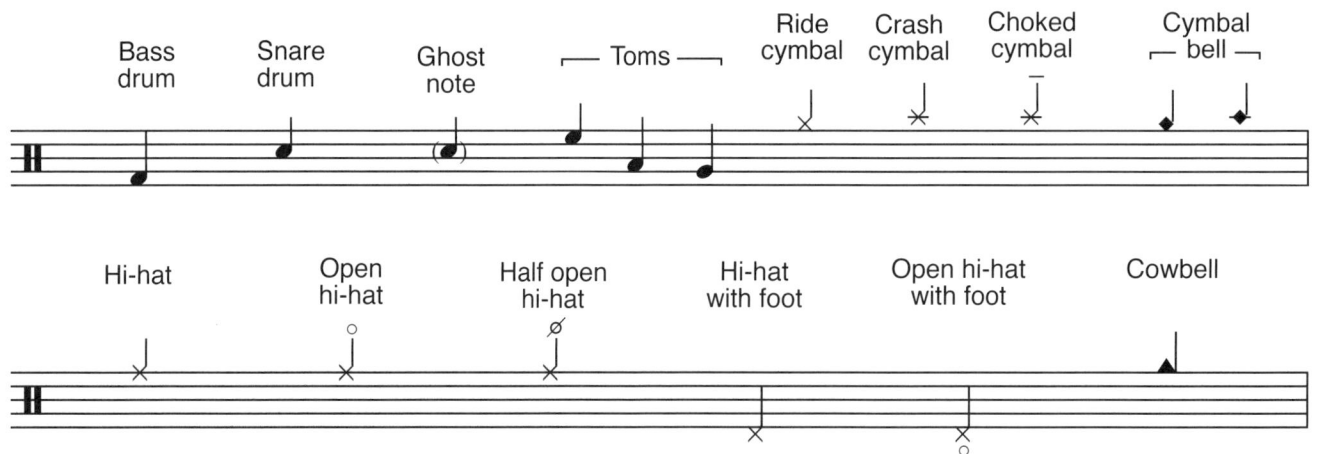

THE SONG REMAINS THE SAME

Words and Music by
JIMMY PAGE and ROBERT PLANT

THE RAIN SONG

Words and Music by
JIMMY PAGE and ROBERT PLANT

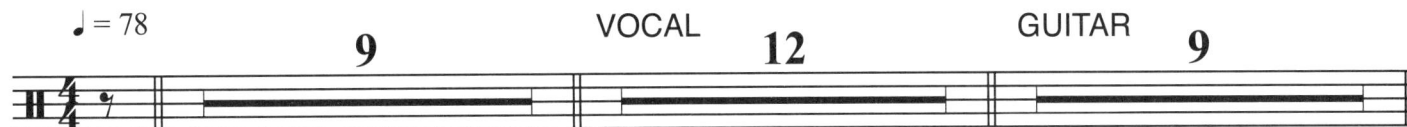
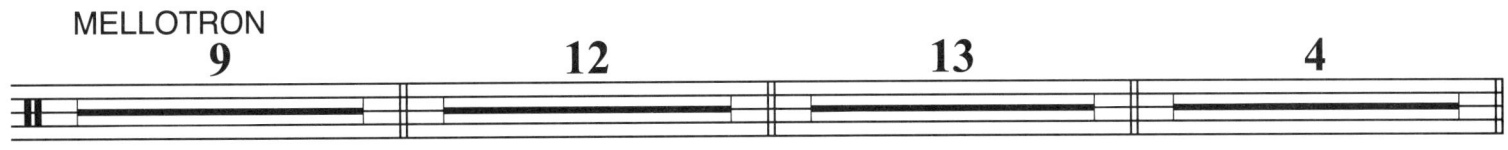
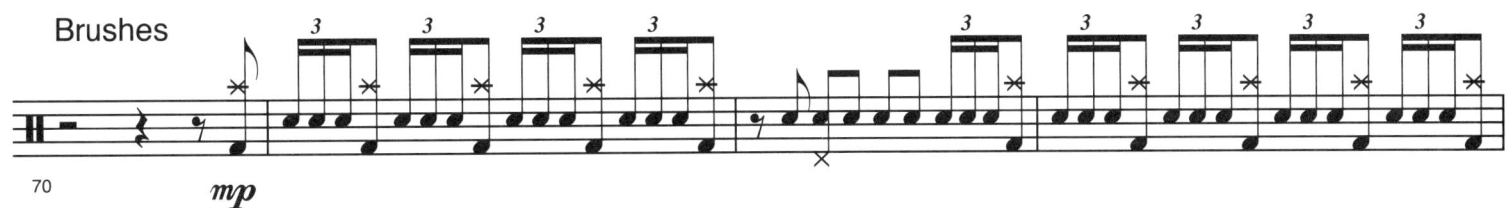

© 1973 (Renewed) FLAMES OF ALBION MUSIC, INC.
All Rights Administered by WB MUSIC CORP.
Exclusive Print Rights for the World Excluding Europe Administered by ALFRED MUSIC PUBLISHING
All Rights Reserved

OVER THE HILLS AND FAR AWAY

Words and Music by
JIMMY PAGE and ROBERT PLANT

THE CRUNGE

**Words and Music by
JOHN BONHAM, JOHN PAUL JONES,
JIMMY PAGE and ROBERT PLANT**

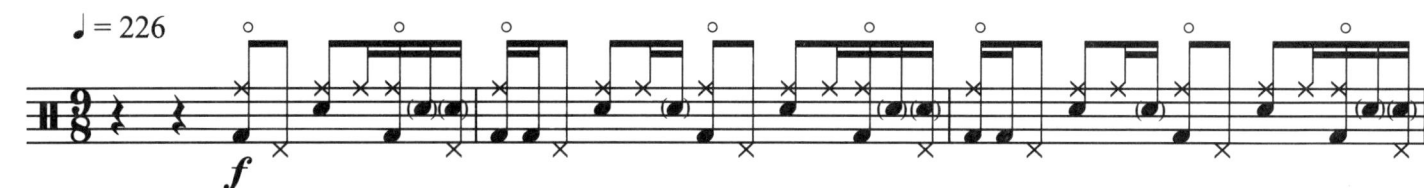

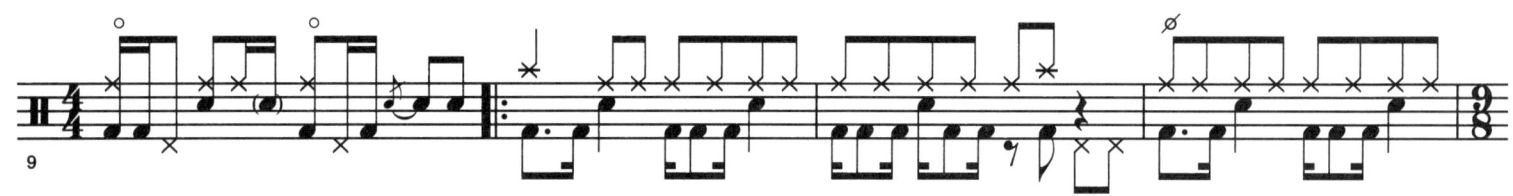
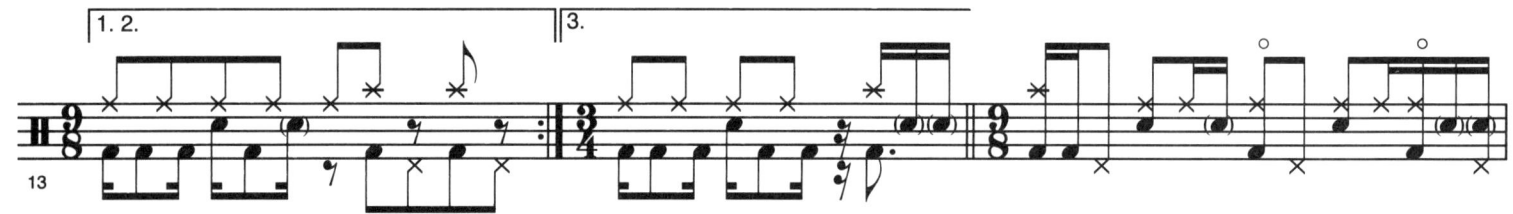

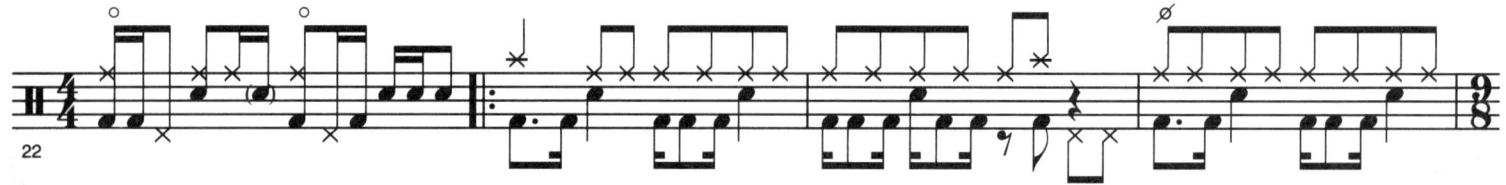

© 1973 (Renewed) FLAMES OF ALBION MUSIC, INC.
All Rights Administered by WB MUSIC CORP.
Exclusive Print Rights for the World Excluding Europe Administered by ALFRED MUSIC PUBLISHING
All Rights Reserved

Dancing Days

Words and Music by
JIMMY PAGE and ROBERT PLANT

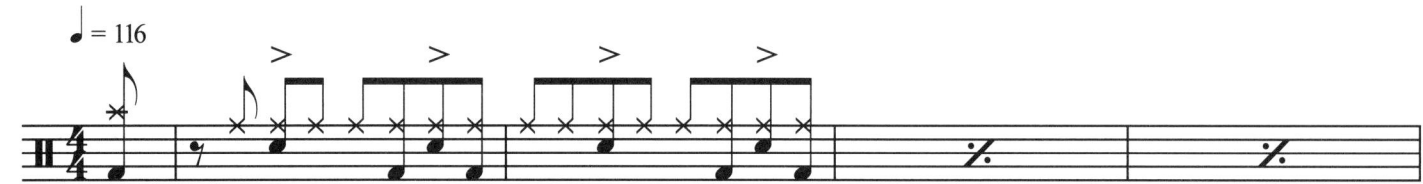
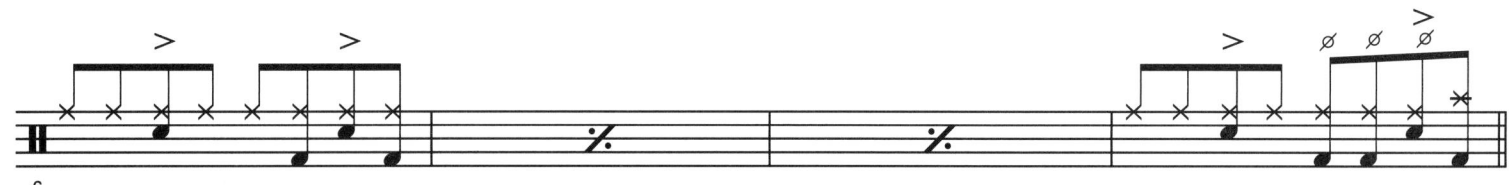
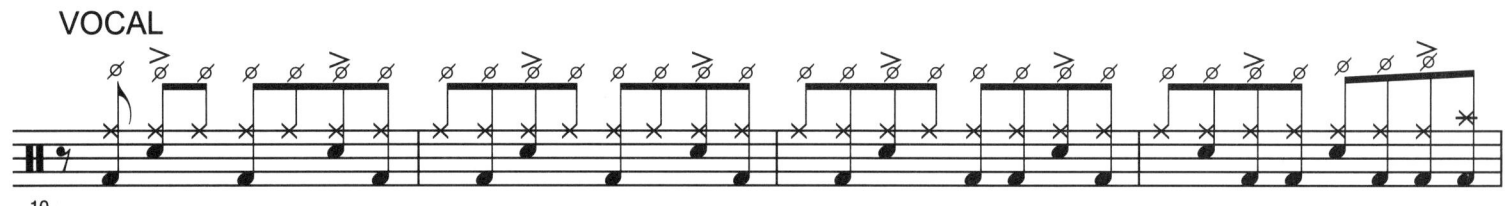
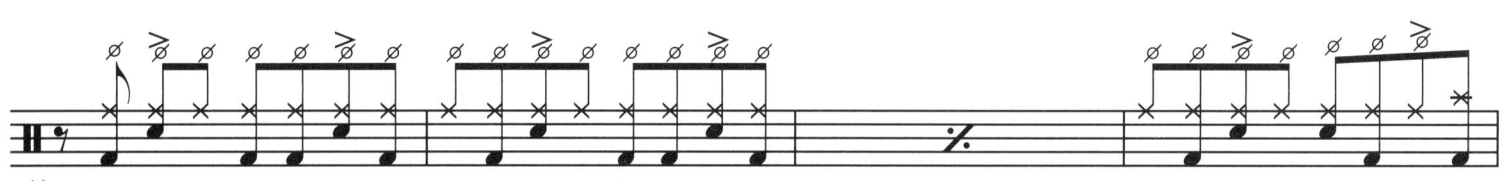
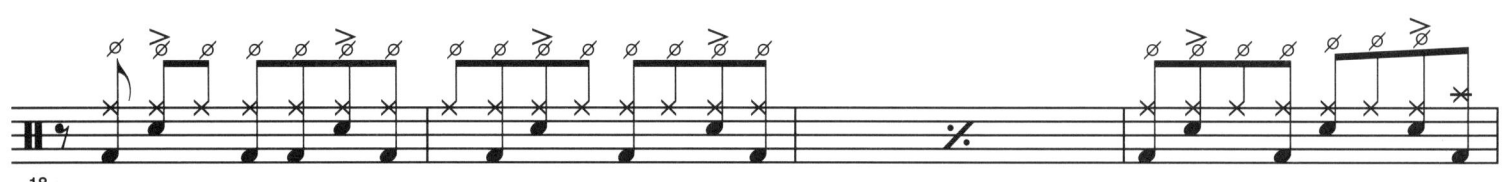
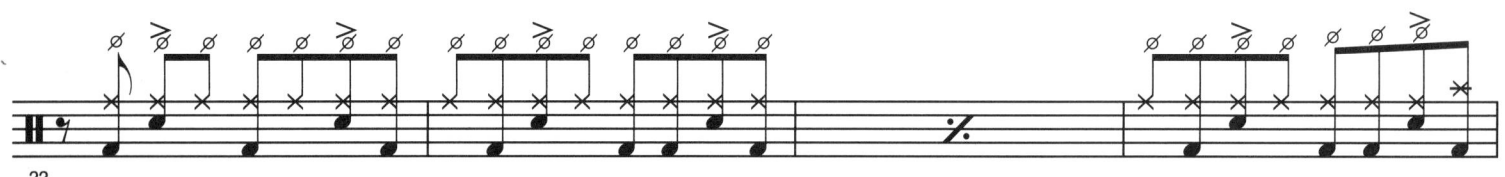

© 1973 (Renewed) FLAMES OF ALBION MUSIC, INC.
All Rights Administered by WB MUSIC CORP.
Exclusive Print Rights for the World Excluding Europe Administered by ALFRED MUSIC PUBLISHING
All Rights Reserved

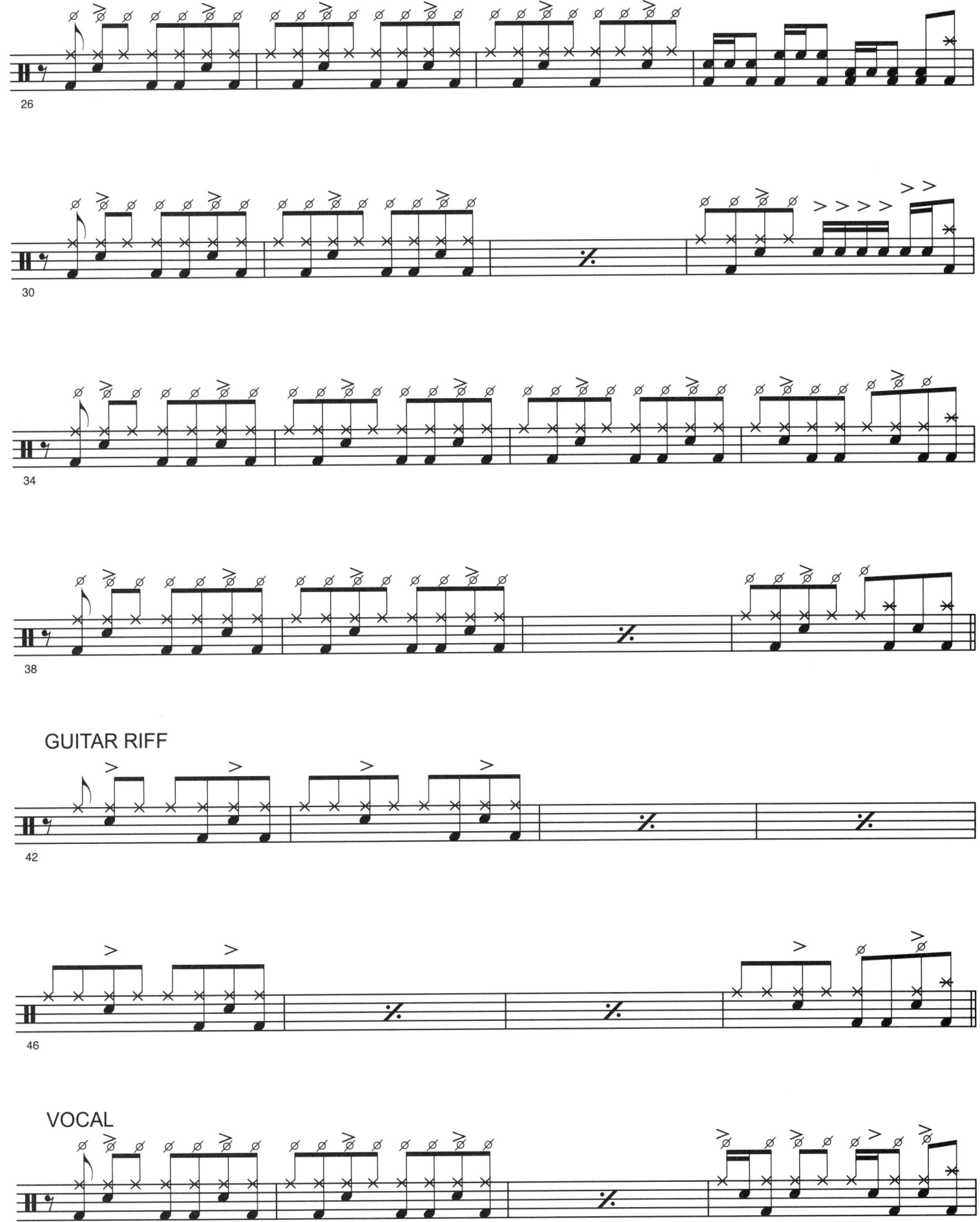

D'YER MAK'ER

**Words and Music by
JIMMY PAGE, JOHN BONHAM,
JOHN PAUL JONES and ROBERT PLANT**

© 1973 (Renewed) FLAMES OF ALBION MUSIC, INC.
All Rights Administered by WB MUSIC CORP.
Exclusive Print Rights for the World Excluding Europe Administered by ALFRED MUSIC PUBLISHING
All Rights Reserved

NO QUARTER

**Words and Music by
JOHN PAUL JONES, JIMMY PAGE
and ROBERT PLANT**

© 1973 (Renewed) FLAMES OF ALBION MUSIC, INC.
All Rights Administered by WB MUSIC CORP.
Exclusive Print Rights for the World Excluding Europe Administered by ALFRED MUSIC PUBLISHING
All Rights Reserved

THE OCEAN

Words and Music by
JOHN BONHAM, JOHN PAUL JONES,
JIMMY PAGE and ROBERT PLANT

© 1973 (Renewed) FLAMES OF ALBION MUSIC, INC.
All Rights Administered by WB MUSIC CORP.
Exclusive Print Rights for the World Excluding Europe Administered by ALFRED MUSIC PUBLISHING
All Rights Reserved